Noirmania

Noirmania
a poem by JoAnna Novak

Noirmania is typeset in Adobe Jenson
Pro and includes discretionary ligatures
after *Phthisiologia: Or, A Treatise of
Consumptions*, a collection of writings
by Richard Morton, M.D., which was a
touchstone for the book's design.

Designed by John Trefry
for Inside the Castle.

This is a text occupying
the expanded field of literature,
from Inside the Castle.
www.insidethecastle.org

ISBN-13: 978-0-9993459-0-0
ISBN-10: 0-9993459-0-7

an Inside the Castle *Loop Edition*

Noirmania

JoAnna Novak

Guilt is perhaps
the most painful companion of death.
—Coco Chanel

I was dead less then   and from the first

joints in my body and brains,   I also lived deep

famine.   I've heard people describe hunger

          as apartmental,   Exodus with

two escalators   white walls, stark over-

whelming windows.   Wrong. In the end

     I only closed curtains, a few feet, this column,

each column,   and I could see

horrified,   the pure white cloth chattered Nothing.

I ran with a word   dribbling black

      from my nose, pink   after rusty

cake, birth   fast and flood. How else

      could anything be? Dusk

with its eye's gold   boredom, floral

      hope in an animal heart.   Let me say

        I was solo, disguised, in four rosariums of rubella

      and champagne, longing to   lose

light, that grub-nailed, grabby, polyandrous thief.

Alone in my throat, evening partied on

      lemon and rung bells   miles from silence.

Shadow was barking and I clutched the ruff, hugging

      for bruises. I found bargeboards. Gates. A mutt

in a wrought pen. And beyond that,   good morning

      incessant glitter.   Good morning,   sole of cherries,

shaky stasis. Good morning, self-reliance,   you

      hound monitor, plate-monger, bell breaker in my fancy

chopshop. This bad   dream had those sticky lips.

It hurts to forget old names. A collar,

a wrinkle, the cheek   drooling over bed is Dusk

I call her, slow pulse, dirge shoulders,

    bosom. Nice bet like me

in the showroom, on the floor. Alive

    it hurts. To fluoresce the gloaming.

To plead, to tomb: I lived normal, a year with excuses,

    sheets, oasis coffee, purpose driving that

mountain. I blinked. Loved doing the blinds at night.

There were many demotions that directed me

       to the house,   where a door the size of the past

waited, unmarked, beyond the tool shed. So I

      thought; I would not lie in a family, unable.

I would not sleep on   my dream. On a porch,

         I froze, heated, thawed—what opposes belief?

Religion means right   the prisoners and rally

      the cure. With dirt   in your pockets,

cry for the children yet cause no alarm.

As warriors lick onions, so my hands

  band meat. In my head, I need more

to tread the boards   and keep the trees'

  stars from wiping out the windshield.

Do figs do this? IVs? Does will beat

  me toward another ring?   Doctors everywhere

swallowing goodness, stepping through

  vomit, marijuana, chalk, oranges.

I do this?   Order all the beef, all the pork.

I thought I should be honored   to be winner

of rose-smoke, and evil. My bad-new

　　　rifle saw a Tuesday.   And I'd only had a

side dish. Deprivation, I   think, is a girl in

Guangdong, London, Carpinteria,

　　　wounded into familiarity.   That was me.

Waiting linked my wrists to the night sky.   To help me see

places, the judge borrowed a needle to poke

　　　the labor. No, it wasn't work   just power.

Feeding was more   missing   than absent from

    my plot, like any nocturnal creature aghast at

        old honey, twerking   twiggery, staunch

    branchlets, painted glass.   Money was the perfume and

        arms were the test strips. All this to promote

    commitment: to the rights of gums, physical

        youth,   a lethargy of sequins and Jello, leaves

    sucked into a bag   and hurricaned over the garden,

where growth was pruned   below promise and precaution.

I talk in the shell of the house, and I like to

    spread the bars of my spine, snore and wait

for never wake-ups, sleep and sleep   and step in

        sleep, shipping out   to drizzles without

        maps. The lantern of possible   wavers.

And a noisy home makes a transparent

        club. It's not so much   a confident

but a cellular sound, patiently gunking

        the bells on every neck and hoof.

It is possible to keep the body

      in bed.   Thin icy fingers, hairless,

reign over my shoulders, a game of don't

      open the fridge.   I know I woke

      in bath, waiting behind a net,

tension nursing my cares. Softly,   I was bitten by

      melancholy. And that was a ledge.   The upper limit of

a village with security, watchers on the seventh floor

      dancing on the feeling of wanting to slip.

I die,   where to die is to touch ground and castle

with flowers on my knees and scurry   for jalapeño popsicles.

Very quickly!   I die and my life is kapow,   a card

on the mantle, a rope round the knob.

In the afternoon, how would it go? Drunk?

In the car?   A nice outfit? After lunch, with a

love? Do you think she reels me back,

to all the dusks in California, in our empty house

with splattered tiles in the new Spanish style?

The problem quacked in my mouth like no summer.

There wasn't a code but black molars,

white honey under my feet. How can a mistake

know about flukes?   Flumes,

combustion, smoke?   Headward I crank now

so stuffy.   Spreeing my passionate mouth.

In its heart teeth

recite the journey, gnashing

without knowing cranberries from confetti.

To learn a dream, asleep   the enemy. Ask:

Is this danger to me?   Do animals and many

birds boast the cause?   In hot weather

does the author recoil from air? As matter accepts the

hoe, so blood   negotiates plasticware, crusts,

brass, steam, paining the skin off the

hand I want. What, humble: turn on me

your clock.   Blink to the house and nod

as heat fears not the sorrows that come.

Hurting for dust, I switched to woods   where maple

         curled into ash,   and wolves marled sheep suits.

    Lift-off meant one leash. Launch, a time-crunch.

All in all a viscid state, home to many a search. (But you knew

     there'd be Dusk.)   And cherubs and gargoyles, herms,

caryatids to ring the last bell.   (This is despair?)

    No, towers and churches and huts.   (Warrens?)

Confines for a shotgun and shine. (Over so soon?)

    And woof: a dog too mute to farewell.

The toy sent   into a fishpond,

    of   bottling kings and reeds

tenders longing in the head.   How quickly

    nobody is lost   silver found to

the floor.   And this, the quarrel

    of grottos.   I wasn't swimming alone, in and out

      but under a helmet of tyrants

    wrapped in a salary. I wasn't following a pull string

but a pulsar,   the gray of small stones in my palms.

The day is so   contagious, a star

    and pretty hair.   So contagious like jumping

Double Dutch, like spikes in the water and

    crowns, like noise   at the harshness of dawn. So

      everywhere like trees and locks,   banks, I love you,

ceilings, toast and more coffee and mountains,

    green and raucous, forever. So spurious the day, so

      stupid. Like a pair of bouncing dice.   Like lunch that hops

from the table.   Like a spill in the soft part of your lap.

From the window one must bank   on reason

          to enter   February by candlelight,

wised up on years and edible

          wax pursing the poppy.   There were things I was

not allowed. Ask.   Will they raise my

          years from now or toss those months to the trash?

                    Like how would I daze in a cave or a mission,

                              mantilla lacing the white of my

          thoughts, massing like clouds over dawn?

And behold   ruddy words I could do!

            Gambling my good luck on an ox.

        The win was a microdrama.   But oh,

            my knees were like apples, pinwheeling

as dueling bouquets or crabs. I can tell you again

            how tense,   to spread a kiss

    for days, to nuzzle   a clinical sex.

        More! More! The antidote is order.

It takes the hair off your brain.

There had been talk,   such blue as comes

    in dreams, silk and wet but solid. The wildest

       sorrows, stopping for sentences—   and these left me especially

empty,   belly waiting for blood vessel

    or a bonnet. I would've eaten a horn. An urchin.

      A weed. A coin.   I would've tried

    but night obvioused the supper, and silence studied

my lostness: a mass in a room in a suite

      off an impossible house with bats and eaves.

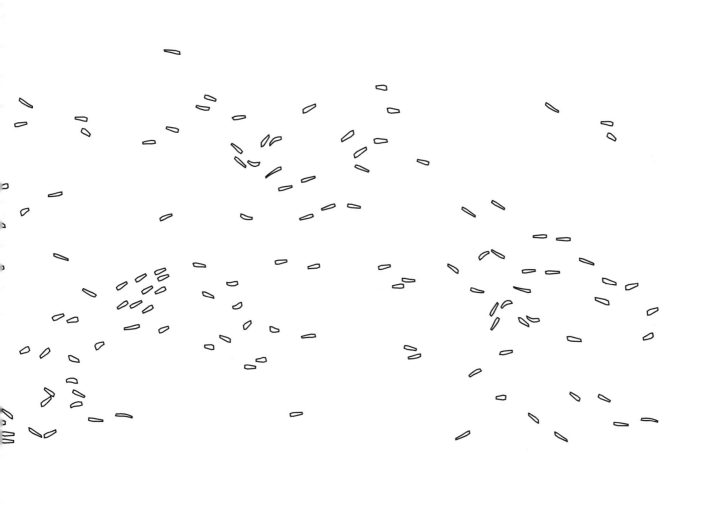

To leave is every   drama. See one

    harried on avenues; bleached   light slices night. That's

evening the score and   flat-lining,   when canula

    causes hungry fox to see canal,   rape of

    fish and fowl, weight in rhythm with man-

  waves, plashy smog and horns

    stitching up the quiet. When I say wound

      I mean want,   a knack teachable as winding

that quasar string   around a dopey button.

If given poor harvest, I grow

    the melting heart, the weaker shoe.   Kneeling

was most days and correct   not present but ordinary

    a way to practice mutation.   One cabin

      a round loaf, butter, persuasion.   I opened

the jar without any assistance and for   hours I watched

    jelly, darken at the swarming of flies.

      Pride was a companion, so   pleasant: to take the heel of bread

and strain   the wine from my mouth.

Yes, yes, I like to solider

  capture gray and matter.   As a child, my side

was wisdom, a serious interest in the hall. So how

  did I draw the door? And what was sitting before

the cup? I would want this day to remain fertile until I ask

  for leave. Then it's prepare the ship and land

    leave notes and daffodils and mushrooms,

  the elegies of mainland people

who examine very carefully   the dark cave called Prevention.

Behold long hands and a curved back,   good for

    busting a shield.   You can also breathe

and dally in black water, find a frolic   at the sink.

    The dusk was rushing   the brim and bowl

until I planted my elbows.   There was a game

        at the lock and a stamping

    in the street, volunteers in perennial garlands.

Maybe it was my butter year,   maybe a dovetail:

    either way,   I drew pints of glory.

Truth on a lifeline is audible   like smoking

    in a dark theater or making a fist   with a grimace.

What I had in gobs was society,

    where tremors confused my   corium,

and let the afternoon crush   me.

    There were lies and I was   spotted,

ready to nova a boat,   jacketing my globoid

    and pointing my naked   nose,

    toward that halcyon stink.

In my head saying goodbye   I guarded

other sights from my course.   The oars were slapping

          and I was so veiny, with food-red lips around

a mountain of thoughts.   Could I paddle

          the question away, skiff off the edge of   brainwaves

and compass myself?   I'm on board

          under deck and taking nothing but trees,

saplings and switches and cuts,   life that will overrule

          me.   Or dry brush that could still fruit.

I miss this sometimes   chewing

    the juice out of youth and   breading

judgement from the others   until stale thoughts

    aghasted me and I had to dash from the table. Who hasn't

eaten alone, at dusk, with the moon

    pouring out like a placemat?   The black cloth

is versatile, like soup or grilled cheese   or pears,

    food you can serve to a child or a dog,

    at a luncheon, a dinner, or a funeral.

Actions upstairs are absent   until the kitchen

     pauses. I yell fire and watch   the knifes drop.

Suddenly everyone's a philosopher   pushing his

     boulder up a mountain,   straining around the dew-zone

     where does countdown from twenty

and watch their fawns gamble.   I've heard the heaving

     is hard, and the deer are sweet, and the sugar

     lumps in your buggy palms.   Then again, I was

sorry: I was inside, barring windows   and couldn't have helped if I tried.

I moved into the universe and   evaluation received

     my type. There were views on   depravity

dark received   with classical manners. So

     simple to curtsey and falsify   gene-work.

       No hatred, but laughter.

No staring, but dulcet   oms. Planets were

     not grown but   broken, tilted like pitchers

     of milk.   The sipping belies

vitality, I heard,   and that's how I claimed the allergy.

We should want hope and bags   rabbits and breasts

carpet and answers and pastures   cows and rocks

trails and jackdaws,   hikers and fathers and barns,

berries and beds, bedsides and nightstands,   bowls of white

sand and jars,   sea glass and gulls locked inside shells

and wicks sewn with begonia and   bergamot like a queen,

harvest.   But if my things can be placed on the floor

do so. Empty the dressers and leave nothing in closets.

Remove the bulbs from the lamps, the books from the shelf.

It's useful to remember

with views of various landscapes.

    and cats, pedestals maybe

the inevitable. So introduce a bounty

    bearable coffins and bespoke trunks.

or pull the teeth from a zipper, but luggage

    This comes with a lifetime warranty.

delicates. Undergarments and vitamins

    roosts inside your body,

fear is a movement

    Say first there are only trees

    help you revere

or a dormer,

    One might worry the latch

    is meant to be hurt.

This net protects

    whatever

anything you'd hate to be without.

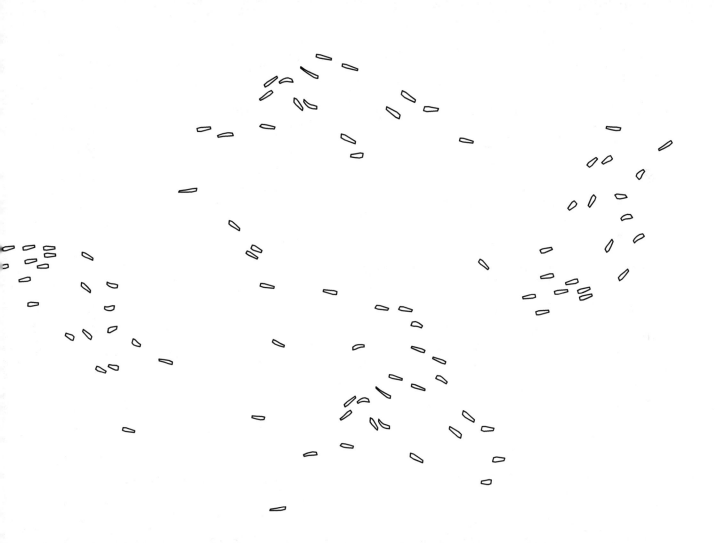

I never remember the beginning   unless I need to

      absent myself from a good thing.   So where did I

find mind to consider my thighs   as marble or deadweight?

      Was I placing the Dresdens under bells or   dusting

        phantasms off a shelf?   Surely I plucked

             feathers from my hope   and watched her

flap around, naked as a vulture in the hot

        nighttime, mean as a vulture   without its flock,

radicalizing its definition   of circle, circle, circle.

I heard alphabets in the megafauna   the days I drove

    myself through cliffs. I was living   on salt

and cemeteries, finding a suitable mound, usual, quiet,

    vanilla, the sort of place that   leaves you with a taste

    like flipping through a book and   dealing straight knowledge.

Absolute.   Bricking.   Cavalier.   Dramaturge.   Edifice.

    Finishment.   Gulch-mother.   Hothead.   Institute.

Jawless, kicker, lastly, mortal.   Nevermore, obit, parsley, queer.

    Rude. Simpleton. Trickbait. Ugh. Verily, wearily, -xteriorally. Years? Zounds.

The end means behind the grind,   so I peck

    chocolate and corn. Nothing is galactic

like twilight, when the showers   are flowers and meteors.

    The test asks you to jump.   Are you ready,

are your ribs right, is your spine   taut?

    I often feel I'll know   the moment and the moment

will miss me, like a dinner at a long table   where the sommelier is

    bad at pours. But that's me, too,   I admit it:

    no such thing   as an empty cellar.

I do not see much right at sundown   when puppies

   swat gnats off my door. Their harnesses   keep them

from cheese and slavering   up my ankles.

   The time is so concrete, I wonder   if I really am

to nod one morning, gone.   Will exit pierce me

   or should   I hold a dog? I could.

I could find one.   Nothing has stopped me from petting

   that saddle, that tail, those ears,   that snout.

Some people don't get along with animals.   That's never been me.

You see the moon sitting at the kitchen table   and how are you

not to judge? So glabrous,   so shiny. It needs blotting

papers and rose lozenges, the kind in the tin   from Adrianna's.

The moon balloons over the table like a memory

of being in a booth, at a highchair   watching the ribbon

around your wrist. The ribbon curled with scissors.   The moon

buoyant with helium.   The meal happy

and milked. A string of red on and on   and up

to a globe obscuring the chandelier,   its hanged lunulae.

Of humble intention, I spread the story　　　　　　good as light

　　　in a barrel of night.　　　Bodies stood and slumped

like feedbags. We had nothing to eat　　　　　in the house,

　　　but I found corners that nourished me,

　　　clarified my urge.　　　You don't crave

until you see pictures　　　　　on the menu: there's one way

　　　to fetishize moods.　　　A photo with oil and

compartments. A pantry of　　　　　measured out

　　　ghosts. The tide-you-over before a car ride　　　when you know the trip will be long.

Softly, if I can   I say, bravely, hey, boy, no.

If you want me, remember   no husbands

       no hearses   no hurtles

no loose collections of recollections.   Dolphins

    you might say, she loved those   their golden

aqua, the doggish grin   of a maw ripped from water.

You'd be wasting good gossip.   I liked prices

   and tickets, splashdowns and infinity

pools, anything   with a scummy white floor.

Only patience asked me to lie

    bodies snug in a spread of light, rolling

        that helps end the box.

and hold up the band: tralala-la-la-la.

    an elastic window with sills

        and each smarter decision

room. The lights hothothot

    people, arriving tens of ways for

        I think.

like four

        witnesses to vanitas

You tip the body

I'll introduce freedom

    for cake

        corridor to a new

and tomorrow, more

you know what

I have it on top, sweet candy   and a finger wet

 with blood. A crop of   arms and a galleria

  of hopes: a leash, a silo, a stable.

My feet grew out from the sheet   and light

 escaped the room.   The dog spoke up

  from under the bed.   The cow jumped over the moon.

Do you end in me forever?   In a house thin as exception.

Can you count on me, hold on me, screw me—no,

 no. It hurts less when you let me go hard.

As I arrived, we were at the beginning

and enemies cutting faces.

up to the stars and the moon.

a tide, latched with crabs and pinkies.

towards a great distance

small rooms with warm wood and soft

I was nothing but metric.

and rings in an envelope, sealed with a rose.

At night some looked at my life. It was books

with family

Someone threw a song

Dusk was swallowing

The pull was

and yet home,

beds.

Some centimeters left

and quilts. Such comforts.

KABINET

With only an **ANIMAL HEART**, the city of industry capitalized on the protein quest. (Source: LEDGERS.) In this way, the abject body was given new purpose.

BELLS isolate the service, which sullies the weekend, when the cantor would rather be splitting biscuits.

BOUNCING DICE louden when the morning is bloated and the ventilation shot. If snake eyes, see BLACK WATER. If double sixer, OLD HONEY. If adjacency, LADDER OF HOPE.

The **BOX** is heart-shaped. It has feet. It stands as tall as a gerbil, but it has no love for timothy hay. Flung at a temple, it should make a mortal dent.

The **BUTTER YEAR** warrants crinolines and sweetheart necklines. To be sure, there are pastilles. Also harpsichords and piccolos, plinking and squeaking a ditty-dirge.

Should a **BUTTON** be placed under the tongue of a woman in her sleep, be certain her dreams will be all fungi and tits.

Brains prone to cannonade under unruly skies must make peace with the parlor.

That **Brass** is everywhere surprised only monarchs, whose ankles assured their soles that every apse and aisle was exclusive. (See Private Ambulance.) Soon, even the bitter seamstresses were threading rattan mats with amber.

A **Card on the Mantle** features the slant-eyed queen, no scepter, a pudgy purse.

Carpenteria will be the site of bloomers caroming off window units, amen.

Frequently, there is **Carpet** for the mourners' fits and falls. A solid is acceptable; a pattern is prefer-able. Choose spots over stripes; fleur-de-lis over saltire.
The rind has been washed in cider and yet relatives can be stupid about everything from station wagons to badges to **Cheese**. (See Gendarme.) To be safe, under-buy.

If the **Clouds Over Dawn** waltz the walkabout, a painful death is not a threat but a promise.

The **Collar** is rarely so heroic, though to laurel it would make a dais of the desk.

A **Coin** on the cornerstone is liberty. Now the purchase of mineral water and lilacs may be considered sanctioned by the universe. Bless her slack purse strings.

CRABS are animals; **CRAB** is meat, sweet, butter-poached. There is something crustacean crawling through a mud of beets. There could be a better fork for this dish, if the garde manger could make up his mind.

The horticulturist's hymn: **CRANBERRIES** dropped must be stomped.

The **CURE** cups the ear of the dog in the courtyard below the balcony occupied by the woman of the manse called failure, failure, failure. (Robed in MOIRE, VOILE, TOILE.)

There is not much to **DAFFODILS**, though good progress has been made in making more out of less.

DOOR THE SIZE OF THE PAST: constructed of veneer and manufactured wood. Gives off strong leather smell; tastes of BERGAMOT and singed orange; fosters delusions of the bourgeois.

DUSK is a thick layer of gesso and a few good rubs with, from, for, and by collected, curious knuckles.

An **EMPTY CELLAR** awaits its elixir, said a lesser epicurean. There should be plenty of level space, shelving if desired, and a stable temperature, for blood prefers the constancy of wool and earth is rarely so cooperative.

Attributed to FINNEUS THE NEVERENDING, **ESCALATORS** work when listing is of no concern.

FEBRUARY BY CANDLELIGHT, or "The Inverness Hare," is a charming aperitif that imparts a chilly mood to the quaffer. Served barely there, in a rocks glass, neat, garnished with white sage bound with coral Santeria cords.

FIGS, five sizes, four colors, three thousand gnats for every one seed.

Early on, the **FLOOR** was seen as a tattered carpet, a last hope. Once the myopia set in, the hen-of-the-woods appeared. See **DESIDER-ATUM**.

With a purging feature called CATHARSIS (now COMPOST), the **FRIDGE** empties itself and begs for its owner like a moribund Italian mutt.

To present **GHOSTS** to the city, a new style of dress should be designed. This is as good an occasion as any to do away with impediments like snaps, zippers, seams, and straps.

GLITTER asks the universe, "why do you do this to me?"

There is no upside-downing **GROTTOS** lest the copulation is double-hinged.

Powdered wigs were once popular, the finishing touch of morticians, but today's elite warrior prefers her **HELMET OF TYRANTS**, sturdy as a rock even when jadish, patina-ed.

The **HERMS** put a blush in the boldest; keep the pugilists in the mosaic gallery.

A **Horn** filled with cream pointing north on the charger, with Malabar coffee and yellow raspberries is morning's memento mori. (Augment with Skull of Small Dove; Bone Demitasse Spoon; Tin of Pitch.) To sugar the day is to suckle abandon until the room tilts.

The **House** should be across from a graveyard, recharged with false doors. See in particular Deady, who lived a life without the cotton gin.

Initially, materializing **Humble Intention** may present a quandary. Oxymoronic though it may be, the concept evokes a strain of postcard-sized gestures that will communicate a posture both hunched over and erect. Visualizing one such gesture as occurring at a cottage table with quilted placemats may put some toast in the toaster.

His fine estate, his drab pond, his Napoleonic lunch—the **Hungry Fox** must wear a starched singlet, a sturdy shade of ivory to offset the gray in his tail.

The **Jello** shall be onyx, charcoal-dusted, a blasted tease.

Yes, women collect **Knives**, too, but rarely with as much vim as men. Find a short stabber or an apple-cheeked pocket variety, red-handled, with useful tools like trim snipping shears.

The **Knob** dribs like an omnibus and sighs the sigh of two hundred jets. (Girls once believed any sound meant someone was pining for their freshness.)

The **Labor** is 17,000 square feet—not even one sconce in the hallway!

The **Lantern of Possibility** is outfitted with an antique brass handle, blemished with sap, oily in places, dark from fingerings. (See **Longeur**.)

A **Lemon** settles the colon, noose of the abdomen. Preferably green, obloquious, firm.

Lips present symptoms of love-sickness, but otherwise best to keep them pinkish and pursed, especially amidst the kissing squeaks of young trees, preening in a moist breeze, after the wake.

Locks will halt the perambulating, not the preening; remember that vanity is eternal and the pavonine soul knows no keyhole too tight, no switch plate too tarnished to act a mirror.

Kept inside a jewelry box inlaid with nicked, rebuffed mother-of-pearl, **Marijuana** serves as a fair deodorizer.

Gabbro **Meteors** plunge into the quarry, monthly if not daily; these should be harvested and used as paperweights, soulweights, and shower fascinators.

MOLARS should be irrigated, boiled, bollixed, gravured—if only!

THE MOON SITTING AT THE KITCHEN TABLE, hewn from shagbark hickory, beside an empty chair, creased with empathy, cross thy heart, along the sea of coal, under a gabled roof, at the home of the deceased, is thirsty for milk.

The **NIGHT SKY** glozes behind daylight. For hours, the earth amuses itself with the gyroscope called heaven; the counterintuitive top, hell.

OLD HONEY lines the stockroom shelves. When a jar breaks, the glass is sticky and the syrup punctuated by crystals. (This is a potion, with a newt.)

ONIONS will speak volumes in a dank kitchen or a wobbly library. Without much effort, buzzards should find them and tearfully extinguish small kill.

For a day the palms will still be malleable: that is the best time to scent them with **PARSLEY**, curly not flat.

For a time it was fashionable to tuck **PEARS** under the waistband, rumpling the cummerbund, but these days there is a wasteland of fruit and the patellae prefer tunics.

PITCHERS OF MILK surround the ewes, who, like their moody, muddy, sturdy farmerettes, enjoy being watched. (See HISTORY OF COFFINRY.)

Once the **PORCH** receives blue beam ceilings (eggshell, linty), it isn't long before the sky, shy, curtsies off stage, flasked.

Cutting a path through the weeds, the **PUPPIES** will sniff out the worms from the landscape, and thankfully they've received their shots. (See THE ALLERGY.)

At the annual festival, a secret harvest of **REEDS** denudes the inner swamp. What these plants do to the spines of young women has long been considered indecent yet highly desirable.

RUBELLA attacks the babyish and the bole weevils. Found in salads, when granite is scarce.

RUSTY CAKE crumbs caramel.

SEQUINS pour from the ear canal when an earwig gives birth. (See DARK THEATER.)

The **SHELL OF THE HOUSE** retains terrier hair and muffin cups and opals, cuff bracelets and a twenty-year-old razor in a silk pouch, cantaloupe-colored, snap-latched, chinoiserie.

SHOTGUN AND SHINE will be delivered by a hangdog scrapple-eater named J- - -X. Keep his toes from the barrel and deliver him a lusty mother.

Long auguring embolism and bad luck, **SPLATTERED TILES**—see CRANBERRIES; see POMEGRANATES—are viscous, moving, taffeta, aril-ed, garnet.

How a **Star** found chandeliering a meaningful pursuit remains a mystery. (Console with Teardrop Crystals; Illumination of Brioche; Payne's Gray Veins Against French Blue Skin.)

A **Suite** is ample and, indeed, it will accost the guest. The spaciousness demands many interrogations: What have I valued? How am I living? Should I own a rug? (See Society.)

Austerity demanded the **Table** be sawed and repurposed. The gentry was rife with opinions and visions: an oval, a pentagon, a parallelogram. "The shape of a beaver's paddle" was one popular proposition; another was "anthill." In the end, the wood was fed into a chipper along with everything else young minds no longer bother with.

What a **Trash** the mourners make of the fairgrounds, scurrying in their broadcloth black, applauding the largest hog.

Twilight has limitations (see Dusk), but the anticipation of a tender-hearted aubaude or a pierced elegy is reason enough to stave off sleep, at all costs. (The Meat of Coconuts may be of use.)

Vitamins may be placed inside a small pewter vase bequeathed by an aunt brought down by wanderlust.

There are grocers who specialize in planks and coals, but this is not a job for men who like cedar. **WARM WOOD** requires a desperate mouth, stuck in the shape of an O.

The **WHITE HONEY** is as big as life and requires not bees but hornets. Use the small gavel, available in the Chippendale, for portioning.

WOLVES prowl the grounds and rouse the roses with their snouts. This may be vicious, ribald, or tender, but carrion is always a matter of petals.

Acknowledgments

John Trefry and Inside the Castle: your vision
inspires and awes me, and I am glad this book has
its home with you.

I am grateful to the editors of *Grimoire* and *Bateau*,
where excerpts of this poem have appeared. My
fondest thanks to Peter Gizzi, Dara Wier, and
Kerri Webster for their guidance, wisdom, and
friendship. Maureen Seaton, Natalie Eilbert,
Johannes Göransson—I am honored to have your
prose on this book.

And to Thomas, foremost, always.

JoAnna Novak is the author of the novel *I Must Have You*. She is a co-founder of the literary journal and chapbook publisher *Tammy*.

Made in the USA
San Bernardino, CA
22 February 2018